Math Sticker Workbooks
Division

Wendy Clemson and David Clemson

Note to parents

This book is part of a program of workbook titles that are designed to support schoolwork and make learning fun. Each page demonstrates a different mathematical concept and provides example calculations. When your child has met each concept and understood it, the practice calculations can be tried.

Many of the questions and puzzles in **Division** are answered with stickers, which are found on the middle two pages of the book. Your child will need plenty of scrap paper to write down the calculations featured on each page before he or she can start to figure out the answers. All answers are provided on page 16.

How to use this book:

The star sign means there is a sticker to put on the page.

Wherever your child needs to fill in an answer, there is a blue box like this one to write in.

The calculator picture appears whenever a calculator is needed to solve a problem.

In the top left-hand corner of each page there is a space for a "reward" sticker. Your child can add it when he or she has completed the puzzles.

D1126868

DK

DK PUBLISHING, INC.

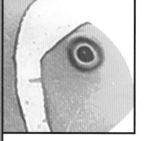

Dividing numbers

Division is repeated subtraction, taking away again and again.
Study the number line to see how division and subtraction connect,
then practice dividing numbers with these fishy calculations.

Number line

Use this number line to see how division
and subtraction are linked.

0 1 2 3 4 5 6 7 8 9 10

To figure out how many 2s
are in 10, you could do the following:

10 - 2 - 2 - 2 - 2 - 2 = 0
There are 5 2s in 10.

Signs and symbols

Division calculations are usually written
out using signs and symbols, as shown
below. Use these signs and symbols to
write out your division problems.

$$10 \div 2 = 5$$

This sign means divide by.

This sign means equals.

This number is the answer.

Dividing groups of fish

A pet store has 18 tropical fish. Solve these
puzzles and find the correct sticker answers.

If the pet store has 3
aquariums, how many fish
fit equally into each one?

If half the fish are
sold, how many fish
will be left?

If the fish are distributed
among 6 children, how many
fish will each child receive?

If the fish are sold in
pairs, how many pairs
can you buy?

If 3 fish are sold, how many
fish will be left in each of
the 3 aquariums?

Leaping fish

Archerfish leap out of the water to catch spiders to eat. If there are 21 spiders and **7** fish in a pond, each fish can have 3 spiders. How many spiders can each fish have in these puzzles?

$$28 \div 7 = \boxed{}$$

Spiders   Fish in the pond   Spiders per fish

$$12 \div 3 = \boxed{}$$

Spiders   Fish in the pond   Spiders per fish

$$30 \div 10 = \boxed{}$$

Spiders   Fish in the pond   Spiders per fish

$$48 \div 8 = \boxed{}$$

Spiders   Fish in the pond   Spiders per fish

Shellfish supper

A group of **60** shellfish divided among a varying number of lionfish. Study the example below, then find the correct sticker answers to solve the problems.

15 shellfish each for $\boxed{4}$ lionfish.

10 shellfish each for lionfish.

30 shellfish each for lionfish.

6 shellfish each for lionfish.

12 shellfish each for lionfish.

20 shellfish each for lionfish.

Division practice

Solve these division problems and fill in the boxes with the correct answers.

$$30 \div 5 = \boxed{}$$

$$35 \div 7 = \boxed{}$$

$$4 = \boxed{} \div 9$$

$$16 = 32 \div \boxed{}$$

$$12 = \boxed{} \div 2$$

$$4 = \boxed{} \div 4$$

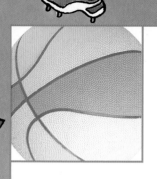

Division practice

Use your division knowledge to see how division and multiplication are connected. Then try these sporty puzzles to test what you know about division.

Relay teams

Multiplication and division are closely connected. We say multiplication is the inverse (opposite) of division. Study the relay-team puzzle to see how they connect.

Can you see how the calculations connect?

There are 20 children to be put into teams of 4 for a relay race.
How many relay teams is that?

$$20 \div 4 = 5$$

To check that your calculation is correct, try it the other way around.

$$4 \times 5 = 20$$

Team players

Imagine you are a sports coach. Use the key below to help you solve these sticker puzzles.

Sport	Number of people in each team
Basketball	5
Hockey	11
Volleyball	6

You can put 66 team players into how many hockey teams?

How many volleyball teams can you put 66 team players into?

You can put 55 team players into how many basketball teams?

How many hockey teams can you put 55 players into?

Tennis balls

Each pack contains 6 tennis balls. Divide up the packs to solve these puzzles.

$$12 \div 6 = \boxed{} \text{ packs}$$

$$42 \div 6 = \boxed{} \text{ packs}$$

$$24 \div 6 = \boxed{} \text{ packs}$$

$$6 \text{ packs} = \boxed{} \div 6$$

$$3 \text{ packs} = \boxed{} \div 6$$

$$9 \text{ packs} = \boxed{} \div 6$$

Game tickets

A family has 12 tickets for a football game.

If the family shares the tickets with other families, how many will each family have?

12 ÷ 6 = ☐

Tickets   Families   Tickets per family

12 ÷ 3 = ☐

Tickets   Families   Tickets per family

12 ÷ 2 = ☐

Tickets   Families   Tickets per family

If they share the tickets as shown below, how many families will receive tickets?

1 = 12 ÷ ☐

Ticket per family   Tickets   Families

3 = 12 ÷ ☐

Tickets per family   Tickets   Families

Sports equipment

Imagine you are a sports coach and have 24 pieces of sports equipment divided up among different numbers of people. Complete these division problems.

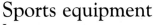

24 ÷ 2 = ☐

24 ÷ 6 = ☐

24 ÷ 8 = ☐

24 ÷ ☐ = 8

24 ÷ ☐ = 6

24 ÷ ☐ = 4

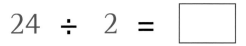

Basketball scores

Below is a list of baskets scored by the star players of 3 teams. Find the stickers to show how many stars each team has.

Team one scores:
12 baskets • 6 by each star player   Stars

Team two scores:
18 baskets • 6 by each star player   Stars

Team three scores:
8 baskets • 2 by each star player   Stars

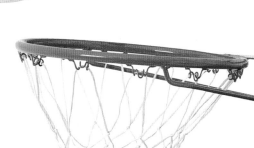

5

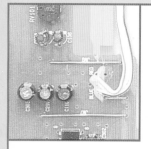

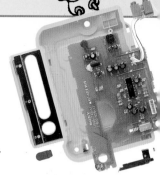

Remainders

Sometimes when we do a division calculation, there are numbers left over. These are called remainders. Do the factory puzzles to figure out some remainders.

Stereo puzzles

A factory is supplied with all the parts to make a personal stereo. If extra parts are supplied, there will be a remainder. Follow the calculation to the right to see how a remainder is figured out.

Study the puzzles below and figure out how many stereos can have a set of 4 buttons and how many will be left over. Fill in the boxes.

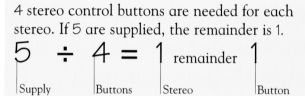

4 stereo control buttons are needed for each stereo. If 5 are supplied, the remainder is 1.

$$5 \div 4 = 1 \text{ remainder } 1$$

| Supply | Buttons per stereo | Stereo | Button left over |

17 **Buttons**

Stereos ☐   Remainder ☐

23 **Buttons**

Stereos ☐   Remainder ☐

9 **Buttons**

Stereos ☐   Remainder ☐

14 **Buttons**

Stereos ☐   Remainder ☐

25 **Buttons**

Stereos ☐   Remainder ☐

35 **Buttons**

Stereos ☐   Remainder ☐

Cassette tapes

Each stereo is sold with 3 cassette tapes. How many tapes will be left over in the following calculations? Find the correct sticker answers.

16 tapes can be divided among ☆ stereos remainder ☆

19 tapes can be divided among ☆ stereos remainder ☆

Transporting stock

The stereos are packed in boxes, and a truck can carry 100 boxes. How many boxes will be left behind at the factory in the calculations below? Solve the puzzles and find the correct sticker answers.

202 boxes will fit into trucks remainder

403 boxes will fit into trucks remainder

222 boxes will fit into trucks remainder

Factory calendar

The factory work is in weekly (Monday–Friday) shifts.

How many complete working weeks are there in the month below?

How many work days remain?

How many complete work-weeks would there in a 31-day month?

How many work days would remain?

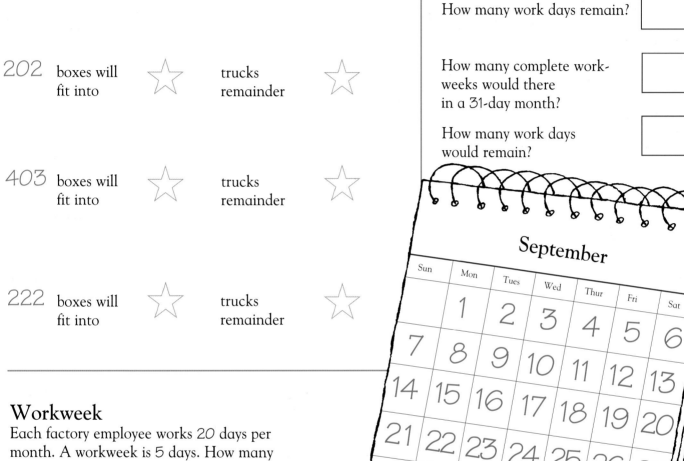

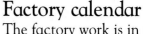
September

Sun	Mon	Tues	Wed	Thur	Fri	Sat
	1	2	3	4	5	6
7	8	9	10	11	12	13
14	15	16	17	18	19	20
21	22	23	24	25	26	27
28	29	30				

Workweek

Each factory employee works 20 days per month. A workweek is 5 days. How many weeks and extra days will these employees work in the following puzzles?

6 days a week for 4 weeks:

 full weeks and extra days.

5 ½ days a week for 4 weeks:

 full weeks and extra days.

5 days a week for 2 weeks and 5 ½ days a week for 2 weeks:

 full weeks and extra days.

Long division

Make short work of dividing large numbers by using long division. Study the examples on this page, then try to solve the long-division puzzles.

Dig divisions

An archaeologist on a dig has collected a box of 345 animal-bone fragments. By using long division, she can divide the bones equally into several groups. Follow the calculations below to see how she can do this.

345 ÷ 6 = ?

Set out the calculation like a long division.

6 | 345
— The answer will go here.
— The figuring out will go here.

First, divide 6 into 34.

```
   5
6 | 345
   30
    4
```
6 goes into 34 five times.

Five times 6. Write 5 on the answer line.

The remainder is 4.

Then, divide 6 into 45.

```
   57 r3
6 | 345
   30
    45
    42
     3
```
Bring the 5 down next to the 4.

6 goes into 45 seven times, remainder 3.

Write 7 remainder 3 on the answer line.

345 ÷ 6 = 57 r3

345 ÷ 11 = ?

Now, follow this long division.

11 | 345
— The answer will go here.
— The figuring out will go here.

First, divide 11 into 34.

```
    3
11 | 345
    33
     1
```
11 goes into 34 three times.

Three times 11. Write 3 on the answer line.

The remainder is 1.

Then, divide 11 into 15.

```
    31 r4
11 | 345
    33
     15
     11
      4
```
Bring the 5 down next to the 1.

11 goes into 15 one time, remainder 4.

Write 1 remainder 4 on the answer line.

345 ÷ 11 = 31 r4

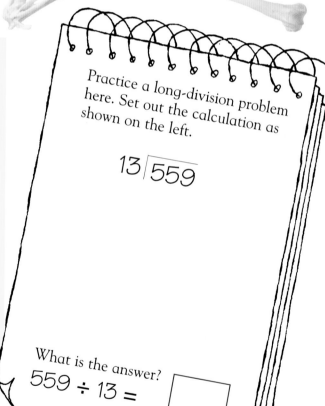

Practice a long-division problem here. Set out the calculation as shown on the left.

13 | 559

What is the answer?

559 ÷ 13 =

Now try to solve these division problems.

350 ÷ 25 =

442 ÷ 17 =

2/3 Dividing numbers
Dividing groups of fish

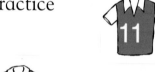

Shellfish supper

3   6

2

5   10

4/5 Division practice
Team players

Basketball scores

6/7 Remainders
Cassette tapes

1   6   5   1

Transporting stock

2   22   2

3   2   4

Work week

4   2   4

4   4   1

9 Approximation
Missing numbers

Approximately 2

Approximately 3

Approximately 5

10/11 Decimals
Partial answers

 0.25
 0.25

 0.75

0.75

Reward stickers
When a page is completed and the answers checked, reward yourself with the right sticker.

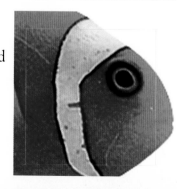

12/13 Percentages and averages

Island map   **Tourist numbers**

12%

2%   15%

13%   15%

6%   89%

20%   5%

25%   10%

14/15 Kite-flying game
Counters

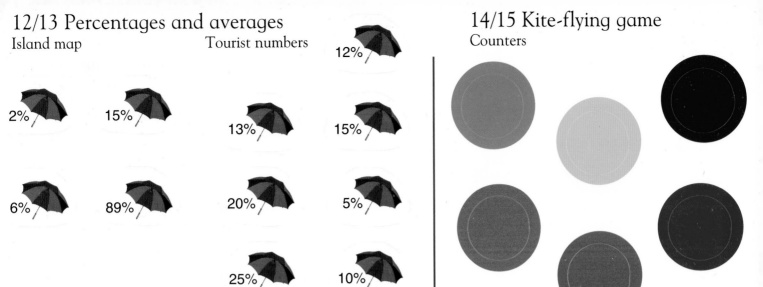

14/15 Kite-flying game
Calculation stickers

4 ÷ 2 = 2	16 ÷ 4 = 4	48 ÷ 6 = 8	99 ÷ 9 = 11
8 ÷ 2 = 4	20 ÷ 4 = 5	35 ÷ 7 = 5	22 ÷ 11 = 2
16 ÷ 2 = 8	28 ÷ 4 = 7	42 ÷ 7 = 6	33 ÷ 11 = 3
18 ÷ 2 = 9	32 ÷ 4 = 8	77 ÷ 7 = 11	44 ÷ 11 = 4
9 ÷ 3 = 3	40 ÷ 4 = 10	24 ÷ 8 = 3	55 ÷ 11 = 5
12 ÷ 3 = 4	25 ÷ 5 = 5	40 ÷ 8 = 5	66 ÷ 11 = 6
15 ÷ 3 = 5	30 ÷ 5 = 6	56 ÷ 8 = 7	24 ÷ 12 = 2
21 ÷ 3 = 7	45 ÷ 5 = 9	27 ÷ 9 = 3	48 ÷ 12 = 4
30 ÷ 3 = 10	18 ÷ 6 = 3	54 ÷ 9 = 6	60 ÷ 12 = 5
36 ÷ 3 = 12	36 ÷ 6 = 6	63 ÷ 9 = 7	72 ÷ 12 = 6

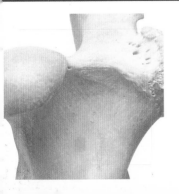
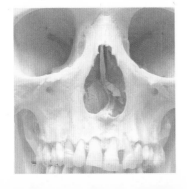

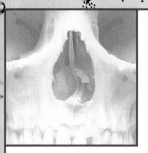

Approximation

Once you feel confident using long division, learn how to approximate. Approximation is knowing roughly what an answer to a problem will be before actually calculating it.

Long-division practice

Study the key below and then practice long division by solving the problems. There will be a remainder in some of these calculations.

Bony facts

The human body has:

206 named bones

26 vertebrae, or bone segments, in a spinal column

24 ribs in a rib cage

27 bones in each hand

26 bones in each foot

An archaeologist has found some bones. Most fit to make complete skeletons. Help her sort them out.

There are 336 ribs.
How many complete skeletons could these fit into?

The 864 hand bones go to make up [ ] pairs of hands.

886 is the foot-bone total.

That is [ ] pairs of feet

[ ] spare bones.

There are 361 vertebrae.

That is [ ] complete spinal columns

[ ] spare bones.

Approximation

Knowing how to approximate helps you check a long-division calculation.

$60 \div 19$ **is approximately** $60 \div 20 = 3$
$60 \div 19$ **is approximately** 3

Write down the approximate answers to these puzzles.

$100 \div$ 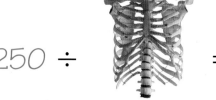 $=$ [ ]
Approximately

Number of hand bones

$250 \div$  $=$ [ ]
Approximately

Number of ribs

Missing numbers

Find the stickers for these approximate answers.

$62 \div 19 =$

$39 \div 19 =$

$149 \div 30 =$

What are the missing numbers in these approximations?

$60 = 3010 \div$ [ ]
Approximately

$99 \div$ [ ] $= 5$
Approximately

Decimals

 Some calculations do not give a whole-number answer. When you use a calculator, you may get a decimal in the answer. Solve these space puzzles to learn how decimals work.

Calculator decimals

Remember that the numbers after a decimal point are parts of a whole number, and the first shows tenths, the next hundreths, the next thousandths, and so on.

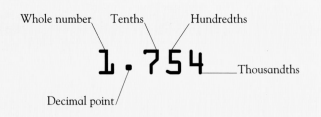

Whole number   Tenths   Hundredths

1.754 ——Thousandths

Decimal point

Calculator practice

Use a calculator to solve these problems. Write in what appears on the calculator display.

$50 \div 0.5 =$ ☐

$500 \div 0.2 =$ ☐

$426 \div 12 =$ ☐

$785 \div 25 =$ ☐

Large decimals

Study the numbers below and see which is the biggest and which is the smallest. Fill in the boxes, marking the biggest number with **1**, the middle number with **2**, and the smallest number with **3**.

50.11 ☐

50.9 ☐

50.01 ☐

Interplanetary travel

Some planets are light-years away. This time-cruncher machine reduces the travel time.

Light years

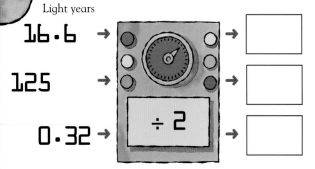

16.6 →

125 →

0.32 →

÷ 2

Fill in the boxes to show how long the trips will take now.

Light years

÷ 100

→ 0.62

→ 0.05

→ 7.3

Fill in the boxes to show how many light-years were put into the time-cruncher machine.

Space buggy

The distance traveled by the space buggy is measured in wheel revolutions. One fuel pack keeps the buggy going for **302** revolutions.

$$453 \div 302 = \boxed{}$$

Revolutions traveled   Revolutions per pack   Number of fuel packs

$$6795 \div 302 = \boxed{}$$

Revolutions traveled   Revolutions per pack   Number of fuel packs

How far will the buggy travel on **16** fuel packs? $\boxed{}$

The buggy's performance changes with the terrain. Fill in these divisions to see how far it travels per fuel pack.

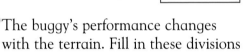

6000 revolutions on **6·25** fuel packs

$$\boxed{} \div \boxed{} = \boxed{}$$

240 revolutions on **0·75** fuel packs

$$\boxed{} \div \boxed{} = \boxed{}$$

Astronaut supplies

This astronaut's snack bag contains **8** snacks. What proportion of the snacks does he eat each time he has **1** snack?

$$1 \div 8 = \boxed{}$$

Remember to write the answers as decimals.

If he eats **3** snacks what proportion of the full bag has he had? $\boxed{}$

Planet samples

A lump of rock is brought back from space and divided equally among **400** laboratories. Fill in the boxes to show the rock parts in decimals.

1 part is   **0·0025**

5 parts are $\boxed{}$

10 parts are $\boxed{}$

100 parts are $\boxed{}$

40 parts are $\boxed{}$

80 parts are $\boxed{}$

Partial answers

Which of these problems has an answer of **0·25**? Sticker the correct answers.

$$23 \div 92 =$$

$$88 \div 22 =$$

$$18 \div 72 =$$

Which of these problems has a divisor of **0·75**? Sticker the correct answers.

$$150 \div = 200$$

$$75 \div = 100$$

$$30 \div = 50$$

Percentages and averages

Sunny Island's tourist office produces many useful statistics for tourists visiting the island. Study these statistics and learn about percentages and averages.

Island map

This map comprises 100 squares. 6 of the map squares show sand dunes. We can say 6 out of 100 squares are sand dunes. Percent means out of 100, so 6 percent of the map is sand dunes.

Study the map key below and count the number of squares on the map that show these symbols:

Squares		Squares	

Now, write in the boxes below what percent of the map this is.

Percent		Percent	

The mathematical sign for per cent is %. Write these numbers as percentages.

12 out of 100 _____

25 out of 100 _____

Map key

 Sand dune   Forest   Airport

 Marshland   Town

Practice calculating percentages by doing these puzzles below and finding the correct sticker answers.

What percentage of the map is covered in marshland?

What percentage of the map is not covered in forest and marshland?

What percentage of the map contains airports?

What percentage of the map is covered in sand dunes and towns?

Tourist numbers

These are the island's visitor numbers for each day in a week.

Monday	600
Tuesday	150
Wednesday	750
Thursday	450
Friday	300
Saturday	360
Sunday	390

 Use a calculator to find the percentage of tourists arriving each day.

This is how it is done:

| Number of tourists in 1 day | ÷ | Number of tourists in 1 week | X | 100 to give a percentage |

Find the correct sticker answer for each problem.

Monday	Tuesday
☆	☆
Wednesday	Thursday
☆	☆
Friday	Saturday
☆	☆
Sunday	
☆	

Average island weather

Here is a record of the number of sunny days the island had each month last year.

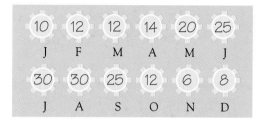

10	12	12	14	20	25
J	F	M	A	M	J
30	30	25	12	6	8
J	A	S	O	N	D

To find the average number of sunny days for each month, do the calculation shown below.

$$204 \div 12 = 17$$

Total number of sunny days ÷ Total number of months = Average number of sunny days each month last year

What was the average number of sunny days a month from May to September?

Average rainfall

The graph below shows last year's rainfall on Sunny Island.

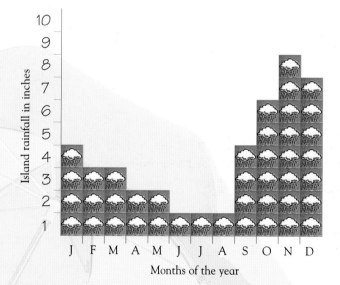

Island rainfall in inches

J F M A M J J A S O N D
Months of the year

What was the average rainfall per month?

Which 4 months are closest to the average?

Of the total annual rainfall, what percentage falls in October, November, and December?

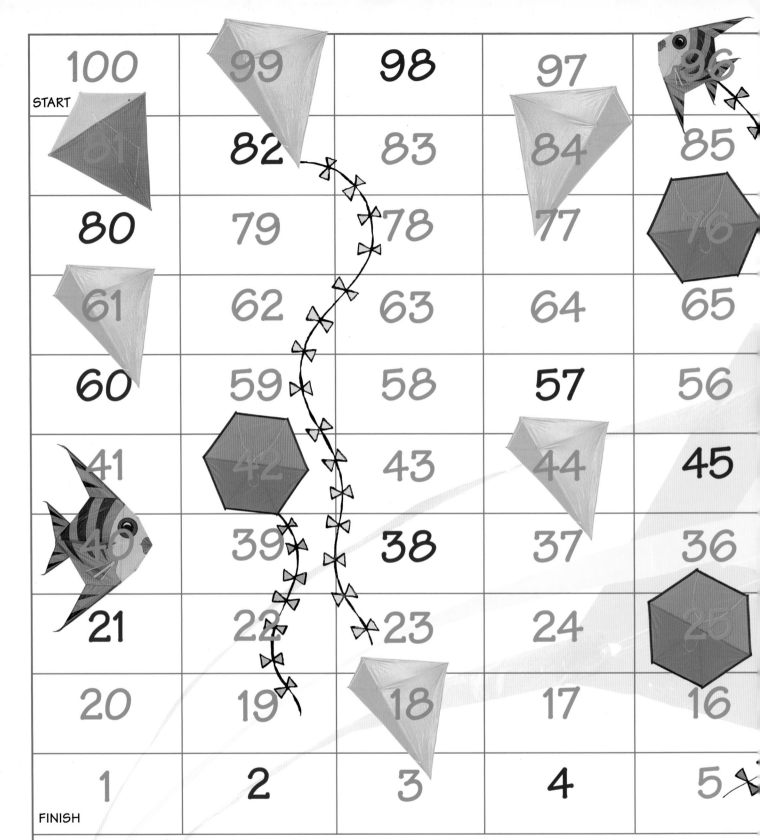

100 START	99	98	97	96
81	82	83	84	85
80	79	78	77	76
61	62	63	64	65
60	59	58	57	56
41	42	43	44	45
40	39	38	37	36
21	22	23	24	25
20	19	18	17	16
1 FINISH	2	3	4	5

Kite-flying game

You will need
- Two or more players
- Thin cardboard
- Scissors
- 1 die
- Counter and calculation stickers
- from the sticker sheet
- Scrap paper to figure out the answers

Making the game pieces
Stick the counter and calculation stickers onto thin cardboard and cut them out.

14

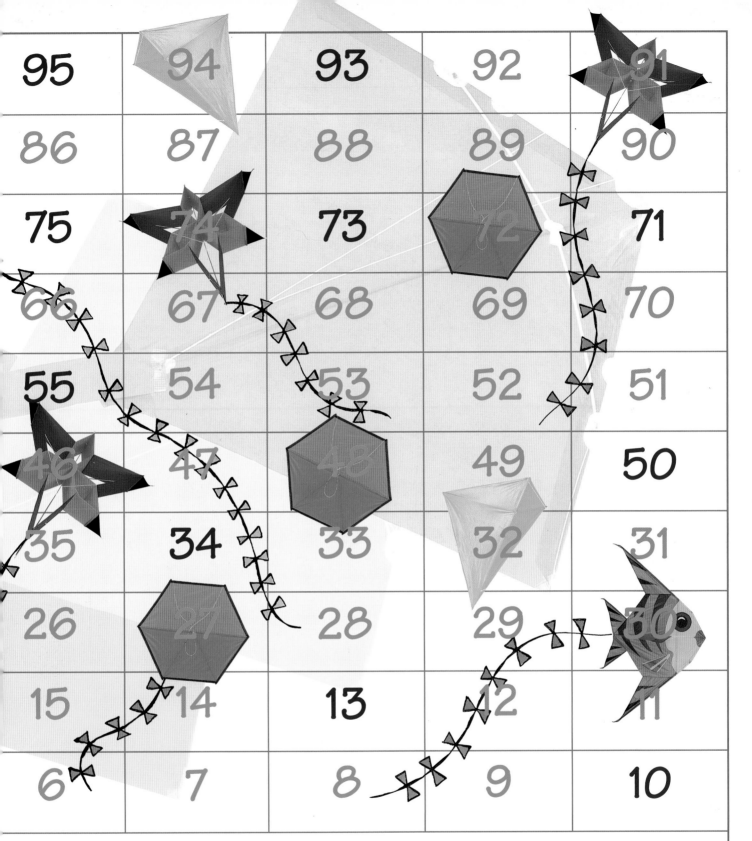

Playing the game

• Players each put a counter on the start square numbered 100 and the calculation cards face-down in a pile.

•Take turns throwing the die and moving your counter along the board the number of spaces indicated.

• If you land on a green number, your opponent reads out a calculation from the pile of calculation cards. If you answer the calculation correctly, take another turn.

• If you land on the end of a kite tail, move your counter back up to where the kite is.

• The winner is the first person to get to the finish square numbered 1.

Answers

Pages 2/3 Dividing numbers

Dividing groups of fish
In 3 aquariums there will be **6** fish in each one:
$18 \div 3 = $ **6**
If half the fish are sold, **9** will be left:
$18 \div 2 = $ **9**
If the fish are distributed among 6 children, each child will receive **3** fish:
$18 \div 6 = $ **3**
If the fish are sold in pairs, there will be **9** pairs: $18 \div 2 = $ **9**
If 3 fish are sold, **5** fish will be left in each aquarium:
$18 - 3 = 15$ $15 \div 3 = $ **5**

Leaping fish
$28 \div 7 = $ **4** $12 \div 3 = $ **4**
$30 \div 10 = $ **3** $48 \div 8 = $ **6**

Shellfish supper
10 shellfish each for **6** lionfish: $60 \div 10 = $ **6**
30 shellfish each for **2** lionfish: $60 \div 30 = $ **2**
6 shellfish each for **10** lionfish: $60 \div 6 = $ **10**
12 shellfish each for **5** lionfish: $60 \div 12 = $ **5**
20 shellfish each for **3** lionfish: $60 \div 20 = $ **3**

Division practice
$30 \div 5 = $ **6** $16 = 32 \div $ **2**
$35 \div 7 = $ **5** $12 = 24 \div $ **2**
4 $= 36 \div 9$ **4** $= 16 \div 4$

Pages 4/5 Division practice

Team players
66 players can go into **6** hockey teams:
$66 \div 11 = $ **6**
66 players can go into **11** volleyball teams:
$66 \div 6 = $ **11**
55 players can go into **11** basketball teams:
$55 \div 5 = $ **11**
55 players can go into **5** hockey teams:
$55 \div 11 = $ **5**

Tennis balls
$12 \div 6 = $ **2**   **6** $= 36 \div 6$
$42 \div 6 = $ **7**   **3** $= 18 \div 6$
$24 \div 6 = $ **4**   **9** $= 54 \div 6$

Game tickets
$12 \div 6 = $ **2** $1 = 12 \div 12$
$12 \div 3 = $ **4** $3 = 12 \div $ **4**
$12 \div 2 = $ **6**

Sports equipment
$24 \div 2 = $ **12** $24 \div 3 = $ **8**
$24 \div 6 = $ **4** $24 \div 4 = $ **6**
$24 \div 8 = $ **3** $24 \div 6 = $ **4**

Basket ball scores
Baskets		By each star player		No. of stars
12	$\div$	6	$=$	**2**
18	$\div$	6	$=$	**3**
8	$\div$	2	$=$	**4**

Pages 6/7 Remainders

Stereo puzzles
$17 = $ **4** remainder **1** $14 = $ **3** remainder **2**
$23 = $ **5** remainder **3** $25 = $ **6** remainder **1**
$9 = $ **2** remainder **1** $35 = $ **8** remainder **3**

Cassette tapes
16 tapes divided among 5 stereos remainder **1**.
19 tapes divided among 6 stereos remainder **1**.

Transporting stock
202 boxes will fit into **2** trucks remainder **2**.
403 boxes will fit into **4** trucks remainder **3**.
222 stereos will fit into **2** trucks remainder **22**.

Factory calendar
There are **4** complete work weeks in this month.
2 work days remain in this month.
There are **4** complete work weeks in a 31-day month.
3 work days remain in a 31-day month.

Work week
6 days a week for 4 weeks: $6 \times 4 = $ **24**
$24 \div 4 = $ **4** full weeks and **4** extra days.
5½ days a week for 4 weeks: $5½ \times 4 = $ **22**
$22 \div 4 = $ **4** full weeks and **2** extra days.
5 days a week for 2 weeks and 5½ days a week for 2 weeks: $5 \times 2 = 10$, $5½ \times 2 = 11$.
$10 + 11 = 21$
$21 \div 4 = $ **4** full weeks and **1** extra day.

Page 8 Long division

Dig divisions
$559 \div 13 = $ **43**
$350 \div 25 = $ **14**
$442 \div 17 = $ **26**

Page 9 Approximation

Bony facts
336 ribs could fit into **14** complete skeletons.
864 hand bones go to make up **16** pairs of hands.
886 foot bones: **17** pairs of feet and **2** spare bones.
361 vertebrae: **13** complete spinal columns and **23** spare bones.

Approximation
$100 \div 27$ hand bones = approximately **4**
$250 \div 24$ ribs = approximately **10**

Missing numbers
$62 \div 19 = $ approximately **3**
$39 \div 19 = $ approximately **2**
$149 \div 30 = $ approximately **5**
Approximately $60 = 3010 \div 50$
$99 \div 20 = $ approximately **5**

Pages 10/11 Decimals

Calculator practice
$50 \div 0.5 = $ **100** $426 \div 12 = $ **35.5**
$500 \div 0.2 = $ **2,500** $785 \div 25 = $ **31.4**

Large decimals
50.11   **2**
50.9   **1**
50.01   **3**

Interplanetary travel
$16.6 \div 2 = $ **8.3** $62 \div 100 = $ **0.62**
$125 \div 2 = $ **62.5** $5 \div 100 = $ **0.05**
$0.32 \div 2 = $ **0.16** $730 \div 100 = $ **..7.3**

Space buggy
$453 \div 302 = $ **1.5** $6,795 \div 302 = $ **22.5**
On 16 fuel packs the buggy travels **4,832** revolutions.
$6,000 \div 6.25 = $ **960** $240 \div 0.75 = $ **320**

Astronaut supplies
$1 \div 8 = $ **0.125**
$3 \div 8 = $ **0.375**

Planet samples
5 parts are $5 \div 400 = $ **0.0125**
10 parts are $10 \div 400 = $ **0.025**
100 parts are $100 \div 400 = $ **0.25**
40 parts are $40 \div 400 = $ **0.1**
80 parts are $80 \div 400 = $ **0.2**

Partial answers
$23 \div 92 = $ **0.25** $150 \div 0.75 = $ **200**
$18 \div 72 = $ **0.25** $75 \div 0.75 = $ **100**

Pages 12/13 Percentages and averages

Island map
5 forest squares = **5** percent
9 town squares = **9** percent
12 out of 100 = **12%**
25 out of 100 = **25%**
6% of the map is marshland.
89% of the map is not forest and marshland.
2% of the map contains airports.
15% of the map is sand dunes and towns.

Tourist numbers
Monday:	$600 \div 3,000 \times 100 = $	**20%**
Tuesday:	$150 \div 3,000 \times 100 = $	**5%**
Wednesday:	$750 \div 3,000 \times 100 = $	**25%**
Thursday:	$450 \div 3,000 \times 100 = $	**15%**
Friday:	$300 \div 3,000 \times 100 = $	**10%**
Saturday:	$360 \div 3,000 \times 100 = $	**12%**
Sunday:	$390 \div 3,000 \times 100 = $	**13%**

Average island weather
The average number of sunny days from May to September was **26**:
$130 \div 5 = $ **26**

Average rainfall
The average rainfall per month is **3.5 in**:
$42 \div 12 = $ **3.5 in**
The 4 months closest to the average are:
January, February, March, and **September**.
50% of the year's rainfall fell in October, November, and December:
Total amount $\div$ Total rainfall x 100 = **50%**
of rainfall in   in 1 year
Oct., Nov.,
and Dec.
$21 \div 42 \times 100 = $ **50%**

A DK PUBLISHING BOOK

Project Editor Patricia Grogan
Designers Kate Eagar and Caroline Potts
Assistant Designer Jacqueline Gooden
Managing Editor Jane Yorke
Managing Art Editor Chris Scollen
US Editor Kristin Ward
Jacket Designer Mark Haygarth
Production Ruth Cobb
Illustrations by Sally Kindberg

Special photography on pages 8–9 by Philip Dowell
Photography by Dave King, Susanna Price, Matthew Ward

First American Edition, 1997
2 4 6 8 10 9 7 5 3 1
Published in the United States by DK Publishing Inc., 95 Madison Avenue,
New York, New York 10016
Visit us on the World Wide Web at http://www.dk.com
Copyright © 1997 Dorling Kindersley Limited, London

A catalog record for this book is available from the Library of Congress.
ISBN 0-7894-2188-7

Color reproduction by Colourscan, Singapore.
Printed and bound in Italy by Graphicom.